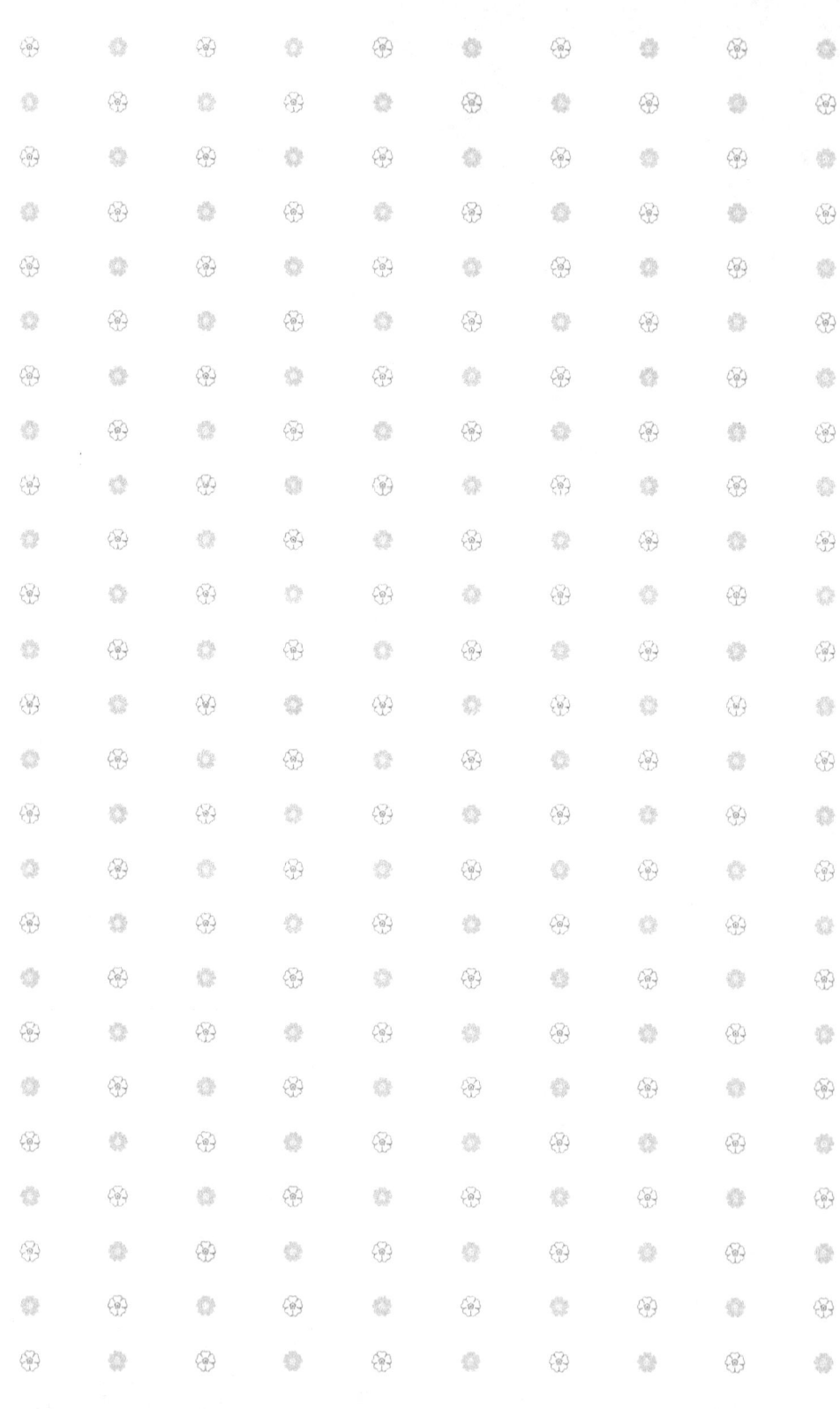

in case of emergency press

We are proud to acknowledge the Traditional Owners of country throughout Australia and to recognise their continuing connection to land, waters, and culture. We pay our respects to their Elders.

We support recognition, reconciliation, and reparation.

Living Fossils are the Happiest Kind

Howard V. Hendrix

in case of emergency press
https://icoe.com.au
Travancore, Victoria
Australia

Published by in case of emergency press 2023

Copyright © Howard V. Hendrix 2023
All rights reserved. Without limiting the rights under copyright reserved above, no part of this publication may be reproduced, stored in or introduced into a database and retrieval system or transmitted in any form or any means (electronic, mechanical, photocopying, recording or otherwise) without the prior written permission of both the owner of copyright and the above publishers.

978-0-6458496-6-0

Cover design: Ward Nikriph

Acknowledgements

"Babel Before Babel" in *Mythic Delirium* Issue #25, October 2011
"Boomer Dog Days" in *Asimov's Magazine* June 2011.
"Bumbershoot" in *Apex and Abyss* First Quarter 2009.
"The Dream Wave of John Scott Russell" in *Asimov's Magazine* Oct/Nov 1999
"Emergent Property" in *Astropoetica* Summer 2011.
"Gingko" in *Asimov's Magazine* November 1994.
"Hemispheres and Atmospheres" in *Star*Line* 33.1, *Journal of the Science Fiction Poetry Association* January/February 2010.
[split pairs] in *Star*Line* 45.4
[city-light cocooned] in *Star*Line* 45.4
[coalmine canaries] in *Star*Line* 46.1
"Memories of Asteroids Near JPL" in *Star*Line* 46.1
[above spinning skies] in *Star*Line* 46.2
"Feathered Eclipse of the Sun" in *Star*Line* 46.2
"Harms of Aggregation" in *Star*Line* 46.3
"After Duprat's Animal Collaborations" in *Star*Line* 46.3
"A Mountain Prayer" as "The High, Hard Way" in *The Mystic Muse* Summer 1987.
"The Symbolic Order in McKinley Grove" in *Poetry Quarterly* Summer 2015.
"Maculata" in *Eye to the Telescope*, Issue #1, May 2011.
"Plaint Of the Stargazer's Spouse" in *Eye to the Telescope*, Issue #1, May 2011.
"Extravehicular Activity" in "Meter" *Scientific American* April 2023.

"On Holiday: Sheep Among Ruins" appeared in somewhat different form in my novel *Standing Wave* (Ace Books, 1998)

Dedication

To the teachers who taught me
to smile seriously at poetry

Table of Contents

Bumbershoot 1
The Fortunate Fall 2
Strange Loop 3
The Siren Song 4
Extravehicular Activity 5
STOR U 4 3V3R 6
The Symbolic Order in McKinley Grove 7
To A Young Science Fiction Writer 8
Zeno's Multiverse 9
Circus Act 10
Emergent Property 11
Butterfly Attractor 12
Canute's Command 13
Boomer Dog Days 14
Plaint Of The Stargazer's Spouse 15
Babel Before Babel 16
Feathered Eclipse of the Sun 17
Stratus Deck, Central Valley (Viewed From Above) 18
The Unseen Good Old Man 19
The Death of the First Person Shooter 20
35 Billion Any Given Day 21
Hemispheres and Atmospheres 22
Climate Song 23
Maculata 24
Felling Cedars 25
Occasional Poem 26
Gingko 27
The Dream Wave of John Scott Russell 28
Plague Poem #3 30
[city-light cocooned] 31
[in tall grass dying] 31
[whitenoise snowblinded] 31

[shooting day for night:]	31
Astronauts Anciently Out of Eden	32
Cicadaean Rhythms	33
We're Precisely Okay	34
Spacer's Chantey	35
Minus One	36
On Holiday: Sheep Among Ruins	37
A Mountain Prayer	38
Greater and Lesser Epiphanies	39
[split pairs have gone a-]	40
[Hokusai's Great Wave]	40
[such skill at putting]	40
[sleep needs dreams]	40
[crater size follows]	40
[trees we thought blossomed for us]	41
[skies cry acid tears—]	41
[coalmine canaries—]	41
[above spinning skies]	42
[for frogs slow to steam]	42
[bird of Avon's make]	42
After Duprat's Animal Collaborations	42
Our House, Earth, Generation Ship	43
Harms of Aggregation	45
Copula for Mathematicians	46
Memory of Asteroids Near JPL	47
Insight Paradox	48
Context Dependent	49
When Encountering Somnambulism	50
How The Preterite Survives	51
Eden's Expressway	52
Another Emergent Property	53
About the Author	**57**

Living Fossils are the Happiest Kind

Howard V. Hendrix

Bumbershoot

Night, a gun-blue umbrella tricked with distant suns and planets,
is not to be opened indoors—more bad luck, or worse.

Hold it to the mind's sky. Finger the trigger in its handle.
A meteor bullets the firmament. The universe falls shut with a whoosh.

Shake the drops of the stars from the loose skin of the darkness.
Think of nothing for which to wish. Step into a different house.

The Fortunate Fall

Adam and Eve departed Eden, letting fall along their way our hopes and dreams—
    worldly goods abandoned by refugees fleeing Paradise's disaster,
    paradoxical undressing of those stumbling toward death's chill embrace
    who did not know they were already naked—

    and so we became human.

Strange Loop

> *"... hold the mirror in hand,*
> *at chest level, and view*
> *the ceiling in reflection."*
>
> from a guide to the Vatican

In his Sistine ceiling,
Michelangelo uncorked
the kleinbottle heart of it all:
a man, in his image, creating God
creating, in His image, a man—
as in Escher's drawing hands,
or nesting Russian dolls.

And the right hand of God
and the left hand of Man
no more grasp each other
than can any hand grasp
its image in the mirror:
intimate gap, infinite abyss
always still to be crossed
by one hand becoming the other

in chiral miracle, or death,
in singularity, or incarnation—
translating all we could only imagine
into something we could only know,
the mind's reach exceeding its grasp
precisely as eternity exceeds time.

The Siren Song

Endtime is ycomen in,
Sirens sing a-doom!
Icecaps melteth, bombers stealtheth,
Soylent green makes room.
Adieu, adieu, sirens sing a-doom!

Neo-plagues make zombie days,
Big space-rocks impact too,
Sun-flares speweth, grid kablooeth,
Volcanoes blacken blue!
Adieu, adieu, sirens sing a-doom:
Adieu, adieu, all someday cometh true!

Extravehicular Activity

Let us stand outside our spacecraft
long enough at height high enough
to see Earth breathing its seasons,
to feel its pulses across years,
the rise and fall of global indices—

vegetation, water vapor, total rainfall,
snow cover, land surface temperature,
net radiation, sea surface temperature—

inhale, influx, diastole,
exhale, efflux, systole.

Is this macro of our microcosm
running a temperature?
Pulse growing more erratic?
Breathing more shallow?

How are we feeling?
How long can we stand
outside our spacecraft?

STOR U 4 3V3R

Moving from a skin long lived in
are you finding it difficult
amid the clutter of memories
lost and forgotten
found and remembered
to distinguish what is not worth
the trouble of keeping
from what is not worth the trouble
of throwing away?

No need to take it all with you
in that final change of address!
Just upload your undecidables
to our virtual self-storage AI
to wait (if the singularity
of being persists beyond
the event horizon of living)
until your decision
shall be reached
or the last trumpet sound
or godhood be achieved
(please don't ask whose)
whichever comes first.

The Symbolic Order in McKinley Grove

Of what is this raven a symbol?

Wedge tail and heavy beak
black eyes and wing beats
swift shadow riding over cinnamon bark
of sequoia trunks massive as pillars
of eternity, returning again and again
of a late May afternoon to a hoarse chorus
of hungry nestlings in her nest inside
a double-holed hollow a hundred feet up:
what is the thing for which this raven stands?
Or is it the thing itself all symbols
fall for, and can never quite catch?

Of what is this raven?

To A Young Science Fiction Writer

What to do, after dreams come true? Remember, Future of the Future,
Never since today has tomorrow looked so yesterday.
Human Edge Detector, bang your head against the walls.
Find a door, get your foot in it, find you're standing on a treadmill.
All a cliché, but with a twist. The twist becomes a cliché, if you're lucky.
A Möbius Highway, going nowhere but taking forever to get there.
Remember to look both ways, aftershock of foretime, foreshock of aftertime.
The world you save may be your own, brokebrain planet that it is.
The most up and coming must turn to down and going, so remember,
Future of the Future, what to do after dreams come true.

Zeno's Multiverse

Whatever became of what might have been?

If answer must be sought in one or more of innumerable universes next door,
If of universes, as of minds, each one is as real to itself as it is virtual to all others,
If to bridge that gap always seems too much yet to be done to do anything at all,
then we end where we would begin, forever just about to change forever—

Zeno hypothesized that nothing can go anywhere unless it's already there,
yet the arrow of time *does* reach the tree of eternity in all its profligate branching.
At right angles to all right angles, forever is only completion unceasing.

Circus Act

The wheel spins, and you're strapped to it—
The knife spins, and I'm blindfolded—

My beautiful assistant, you never look at me
from this place where I'm not seeing you,
but we both know, *mon semblable*,
our show goes on only so long
as I keep throwing my knives
      again! again! again!
and you keep missing the point
      again! again! again!
as closely as possible.

The last knife, the hardest throw—
Wait for it—

To let us go.

Emergent Property

The astronomer, separating the "signal" of shower-associated meteors from the
    "noise" of sporadic meteor background, does not ask whether the mind
    conjures constellations out of the stars, or the stars conjure constellations
    out of the mind. Her fleeting scratches of light, caught by motion-triggered
    video cameras, make stars constellated by imagination seem solid
    as the keystone in heaven's arch.

She knows the old Arabic tale: shooting stars are stones thrown by angels at afreets
    eavesdropping on the secret counsels of heaven. In previous lives or alternate
    universes were all meteor-shower astronomers enormous skulking demons stoned
    on shooting stars and heavenly secrets? She wonders. Perhaps it is to appease
    our inner demons that we spend our time searching out creatures from the Id:
    Draconids. Hydrids. Cygnids. Leonids. Taurids. Ursids. Et ceterids.

Her colleagues have used that joke against her, but when she's done subtracting from
    the daily background of sporadics all known meteors associated with named
    showers, she thinks she'll name what's left—the "shower" of all meteors which are
    not part of named showers—"Ephemerids," just to annoy them with the logic of it.

They consider her an irritant, but it is sand makes oyster grow pearl,
    stone makes air grow meteor, noise makes message grow signal—
    and not too much to imagine meaningful dreams and nightmares
    might flash from anywhere in the sky, anytime.

Living Fossils are the Happiest Kind

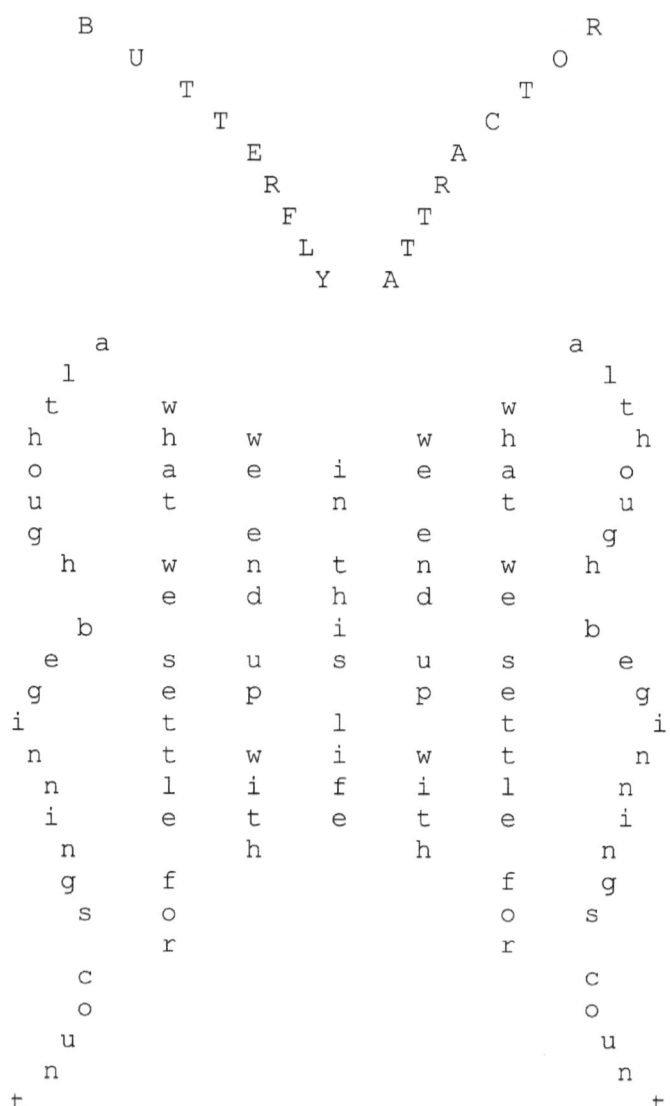

Canute's Command

they do not speak like we do
they do not follow orders
the damned migrant butterflies
have no respect for borders

the field-flitting monarchs
of canada, america, mexico
must learn it's only capital
can freely ebb and freely flow

send up the micro-drones
with their wasp-missile stings
we'll teach these insects boundaries
beyond the borders of their wings

Boomer Dog Days

we drink our wine from a corporate satellite
we knock back our cocktails via geosynchronous orbit
we smoke our weed captioned with the date
and US Eastern Daylight Time
to Sirius XM's '60s-'70s
mellow rock "The Bridge" playing
almost imperceptibly
and dream we still understand
what the space race was all about
as, one down from the NASA channel,
DISH Earth on our TV package
shows to that music a view of a planet
over which an occulting shadow steals
almost imperceptibly

Plaint Of The Stargazer's Spouse

for Bruce Boston

Your thoughts swim so long
amid the night sky's distant lights
I wonder you don't need to jump
up and down on either foot
or bang the opposite side of your head
with the palm of your opposite hand
to get the shooting stars out of your ears.

Babel Before Babel

the zoo animals endlessly
screech roar howl bray bellow bay
I am my keeper's brother!
I am my keeper's brother!
but the bane of tongues
keeps the keeper from understanding
a sin more ancient than Cain's

Living Fossils are the Happiest Kind

Feathered Eclipse of the Sun

(...clouds of birds that could block out the sky for hours or even days...)

our language was song
until you taught us to speak—
curse your cursing us

                                      uplifting our minds
                    until they soared with your wings
                          and, ungrateful us,

demanding return—
of dodos, pigeons past count,
to flock with life's brood—

                              museums, give back
                          our dinosaur ancestors'
                      bones we claim for ours;

universities,
unstuff your fat collections
let them fly your coops

                            let feathered eclipse
                    top eclipse of the feathered
                            with murmuration

Stratus Deck, Central Valley (Viewed From Above)

Having snowshoed Eagle Trail through pines and firs, we stand at 8,000 feet
    under skies empty of eagles but not of two ravens showing off amid thermals
    above spare wind-twisted trees on granite domes.

An inland sea of fog and cloud 3,000 feet deep fills the San Joaquin Valley below,
    stratus deck making a lost Atlantis of Fresno, blue islands of foothills' tops,
    a far-off country of the Coastal Range.

Through vast blue bubble of high pressure weather a jet too high to see
    scratches a pale contrail line, its streak of white vapor above us
    casting a broad grey shadow upon the ocean of white vapor below.

Evanescent as snowshoe tracks in sun, maps of lost cities,
    cloud chamber traces from the smash-ups of atoms,
    word-shadows cast by streaks of thought
    inside a bubble of skull—is that shadow of trail there
    all we know of the way home?

The Unseen Good Old Man

The older I get, the smaller the stride I make
until, one day, I shall walk with the shuffling gait
of someone feeling, foot by foot, the way
through a darkened house, anxious not to stub a toe
on death, or trip on the bottom step of heaven

Living Fossils are the Happiest Kind

The Death of the First Person Shooter

From timeless deep I fell into the beat
Run gun zero one forget about oblivion
Pixel skies so much wider than my dreams
When I died they unplugged me from machines

35 Billion Any Given Day

poultry numbers mean
when the Planet Eater comes
Earth tastes like chicken

Hemispheres and Atmospheres

the sunlit side of the brain chews into grammar
the howl rising from the moonlit side of the mind

with the first drops of that dark storm's rain
puffs of dust leap from parched tongue

language is the dry shadow
third eye eclipsed by invisible hand
when for all my words cannot say
I stand, in the way

Climate Song

Hard winters make for easy summers,
Hard winters make for easy summers.
You know when it's snowing like hell,
Come summer there's water in the well.
Hard winters make for easy summers,
Hard winters make for easy summers.
We're all born into the same sky,
But in many weathers we will die.
Hard winters make for easy summers,
Hard winters make for easy summers.
The high mountains where I live
Can't forget, but they will forgive
and every spring is forgiveness.
Hard winters make for easy summers,
Hard winters make for easy summers.

Maculata

Under the aspect of an oil-soaked otter eating a sea urchin, the sea priest breaks over his heart his bread of thorns for her.

He places on her tongue all the tears of the ocean, transubstantiated to orange gobbet of urchin flesh. She tastes winter evenings on forgotten beaches.

The tide, a broken promise, a gentle lie, whispers with a soft hiss, departing.
She rises from the altar of waves, heading inland, the sea in her belly.

Felling Cedars

Pink blood overflows the bar-oil reservoir. The gas/oil mix tank is blackeye full. The saw chain, teeth sharp enough to catch and cut, must be tight (but not too tight) on the cutting bar. I am careful of my hands.

With a screwdriver I tighten the tank caps into place. I grip and yank the pull cord until the engine grumbles to life. Biting into the trunk the saw spits out a plume of cedar shavings like a classroom's worth of pencils all run through the sharpener at once.

The gibbous moon of wood the saw chews out, a Humboldt cut, makes a toothless pumpkin smile on the side where I want the tree to fall. Coming round behind the trunk, biting the saw in on a line even with the top lip of that lipless smile, I am too aware the idiot machine will chew flesh and bone as soon as bark and heartwood. My head conjures hot dark scarlet of extremities severing, torment of hand or foot already lost—pain of phantom limb, stump hallucination, map in the brain insisting the country of the lost hand is still there, despite all the eyes' denials.

My free (and still intact) gloved hand pushes on the trunk that's now almost cut through. I lean into it, sending the cedar creaking over, falling through air with a woosh of branches, hitting ground with a thudding crash. Severing its limbs for slash, sawing the trunk to stove lengths for drying and splitting, I stare a moment at the abandoned tree stump. As it dies, does it hallucinate trunk and limbs and green solar needles, all still shining in the tall wind?

Then I know. Both feller and tree may fall victim to the steel-toothed machine, but only the tree will be innocent.

Occasional Poem

For roof and sky overhead
For drink and food by which we're fed
For loves we don't forget
For friends absent or still unmet
What more need be said?
      Save thanks, thanks, thanks.

Gingko

your leaves fall
two hundred twenty million years ago
fans of endearing maidens
pressed between pages of coal

beneath your boughs strut the lucky dragons
but no boneshadows record
the color of crushed dreams in their eyes
when their fortunes change

you grow weary, dwindle toward sleep
until the awakening priests come to plant you
in the Pure Land of their temple gardens
that those who may not eat meat may eat of you

men of science snatch you from the temple precincts
a new geisha to join their harems
coelacanth and nautilus and platypus and you
the most hopeful fossils are those still living

out of love we plant you beside our stone roads
to inhale our burning smoke, to exhale your sweet air
you are patient, so patient you do not worry
who will love you after we are gone

The Dream Wave of John Scott Russell

The body is a horse-drawn boat moving up a canal. In sleep the boat stops,
> but the water in the canal doesn't.

Dreaming is involved in memory and learning.

Wake becomes wave, rounded, smooth, well defined, unwavering.

Deprive people of their dreams and they don't organize what they've perceived—
> they don't learn.

In August 1834, John Scott Russell, engineer on horseback, rides beside the Union Canal
> for miles, keeping pace with a strange solitary swell,
> started when a horse-drawn boat
> stopped.

Dreaming organizes what has already been perceived; at times it also organizes what is yet
> to be perceived.

The wave is full of tiny, innumerable faces. Phase-locked, wave-coupled, entranced,
> Russell dares not interfere with this channel surge that
> refuses to disorganize itself.

A precognitive dream may be regarded as a memory of what is yet to be.

When a tall thin example of what Russell calls a solitary wave catches up with a shorter fatter

> variant of the same, the two waves merge and coalesce completely into one.

The sleep of dreams is the most fractal. Wake the sleeper and the wave collapses.

Time disappears in the deep waters behind as the wave of faces rolls away.
> Russell builds a wave tank in his garden, works with barges on the canal,
> uses his solitary waves to correctly calculate the depth of the atmosphere.
> He dreams of one day using solitary waves to determine the size of the universe.

Eventually the two waves emerge intact, the tall thin one racing ahead, the short fat one
> falling behind, remembering their former organization through a species of nonlinear
> memory.

In the windings of the channel Russell loses the wave. The wave, however, never loses him.
> Least of all when his horses and boats stop.

Plague Poem #3

Self-isolation is nothing new.

Each of us gets so caught up in our own little world
we forget everybody else is caught up
in their own little worlds as well,

when we are all of us together in this one big world
which in the grand scheme of the universe
is such a little world, too.

[city-light cocooned]

city-light cocooned
worms, tear open too-bright dark—
emerge moths to stars!

[in tall grass dying]

in tall grass dying
crickets lament worlds undone
autumn evensong

[whitenoise snowblinded]

whitenoise snowblinded
Digital Man still finds death
without GPS

[shooting day for night:]

shooting day for night:
snowflakes falling through sunshine
winter meteors

Astronauts Anciently Out of Eden

if naked to the invisible eye from space
all of us ever since Adam from Eve
saw that they were
and everybody was
as the voice still on legs hissed
who told us that waking
is falling short of falling
asleep while dreaming
then why did the other voice boom
Who told you that? like it didn't know—

just asking—was He just asking?
always got to watch our step
when orbit like walking is
falling short of falling
on two legs to the moon
sufficient to have stood
yet free to fall
upon its peaks
of eternal light

Cicadaean Rhythms

After seventeen years' burial, we the undead climb out of the
ground onto tree trunk,
> porch post, work bench. Fastened in slow zombie pounce
> on dull uprighteousness,
> skin popping we burst from our own backs, writhing free
> our crumpled cellophane wings,
> our packing-peanut meat, until—filling out, firming up—
> red-eyed, black-bodied, glittering
> —we buzz you.

Machineries of insect joy whirring love-noise symphonies, we
are Saint Valentine's
> and Halloween met in midsummer day-scream, fashioned
> by a shade-tree Shakespeare
> to frighten your little ones.

We're Precisely Okay

"Okay" is okay; "OK" is okay, "okay" is okay,
but "Ok" is not okay and "ok" is not okay—
both look like they sound like
the name of a largish extinct flightless
North Atlantic bird, or the last syllable
of recorded time in one word from one language
for the gods in their twilight years—
both of which we increasingly resemble
in too many ways: two aging English professors
who, knowing our plurals from our possessives
(orthographically, grammatically, romantically),
have learned enough to remain number-shifted
from two to some kind of one.

Spacer's Chantey

(A Fragment, for Joe Haldeman)

Home, for a star
in the naked-eye sky,
is best viewed from not far
past the orbit of Mars.
But way out where war's fought
you can't see that blue dot
unless you use a deep scope,
which might well dampen your hope
of getting home from the stars,
ever coming home from the stars.

Minus One

heat speeds daffodils
no time for budding flowers
to rest from blooming

rope-slung bald tire swings
seventeen-year-old lovers
through cicada song

fallen leaves imprint
concrete before it hardens
or so parents hope

felled, cut in rounds, split,
sunlight of sap-risen days
flares in snow-roofed hearths

daffodils turn cicadas turn
fallen leaves turn snow-roofed hearths
turn years

haiku, locusts, us,
prove in syllables as time:
our last end is prime

On Holiday: Sheep Among Ruins

Battlefields become bus stops. Massacres melt into folksongs,
freeze into marble.
The king divorces, the abbey dissolves. Yesterday's cathedral becomes
this morning's rock quarry.

We sheep don't care. Ancient stones conspire in silence on
a windswept plain.
Their secrets are safe. We have other concerns: Consume that grass,
produce that wool! No fleece without dags, no dags without fleece!

With lambs to bounce teats at lambing time, all are perfectly content—
so long as, now and then, we get to rub our shaggy flanks
up against a monument.

A Mountain Prayer

O Shaper beyond all shapes who dwells in every shape:
>With the mellowing geometries of these proud humble mountains,
>shape me.

O Light beyond all lights who dwells in every light:
>With the starsplashed night, with the warm star of day,
>light my way.

O Sound beyond all sounds who dwells in every sound:
>With the air-ocean whisper of the high pine wind,
>resound in me.

O Teacher beyond all teachers who dwells in all that teaches:
>Teach me the truths of forever to be seen in a single day.
>
>Teach me your high hard way.

Greater and Lesser Epiphanies

At moving final scenes on stage or screen or page, stiff-lipped old men cry easier.
    Endings grow particular with those living closer to life's close.
    By such reasoning old women should cry easier too, but I won't presume to say,
    no matter how much these old man's tears may make an old woman of me.

But no. Tears alone cannot epitomize creatures who epiphanize—

For minds opening like infinite petals of an eternal rose, Time is vertigo of eternity,
    illusion of history's motion in what is always already everywhen all at once!
    Space is dizziness of infinity, off-kilter mirage of one thing discrete from another,
    and another, in what is always already all one thing, playing at everything!

For minds opening like an eternal rose of infinite petals, boundless timeless oneness
    is the all in all, in which all multiplicities, all endings, all beginnings, all boundaries
    participate!

True, true, all true. What blows our minds can dry our eyes, but greater epiphanies
    don't make the lesser any less true: That the dizziness we love when young
    is the vertigo we fear when old, or at moving final scenes on stage, screen, page,
    old men cry easier, perhaps old women too, for all the best of our good reasons,
    under the rose.

[split pairs have gone a-]

split pairs have gone a-
Hawking, singularity's
center cannot hold

[Hokusai's Great Wave]

Hokusai's Great Wave,
oak limned branch and twig with snow—
fractal synchrony

[such skill at putting]

such skill at putting
this foot in my mouth makes this
tongue fit for a shoe.

[sleep needs dreams]

sleep needs dreams as dark
needs stars—close your eyes to see
their constellations!

[crater size follows]

crater size follows
Zipf's law down Moon Rabbit holes—
Pareidolia?

[trees we thought blossomed for us]

trees we thought blossomed for us
still bloom for themselves

seas we thought raged against us
still roar for themselves

words we thought spoken by us
still speak for themselves

worlds we thought were made for us
still turn for themselves

stars we thought shone down for us
still shine for themselves

after we are gone

[skies cry acid tears—]

skies cry acid tears—
on drowned floors of rising seas
mother of pearl weeps

[coalmine canaries—]

coalmine canaries—
music intentionally
overwhelmed with noise

[above spinning skies]

above spinning skies
homesick vertigo selfie
of our place in space

[for frogs slow to steam]

for frogs slow to steam
changeless hope is dangerous
past all *jump!* of fear

[bird of Avon's make]

bird of Avon's make
rude mechanical of song
warbles woodnotes wild

After Duprat's Animal Collaborations

caddis worms of text
AIs prompted weave cento
with worldwide web(s)ilk

Our House, Earth, Generation Ship

I.

granted our gen ship was never an ark—
when we native invasives appeared
other species disappeared
that was our magic trick
we appeared they disappeared
before our very eyes
often vanishing
before our very eyes
had even noticed what we
unconscious magicians
had already rendered
inconspicuously absent

II.

300,000 years to get the first billion human passengers aboard
until in our lifetimes boarding soared to a billion every 12 years
loading 25,000 times faster than our baseline passenger capacity
speed of a brisk walk becoming fast as the Juno spacecraft

III.

this is just to say that like everyone we thought we were safe from disaster
until we weren't and we found ourselves happy to be inside falling star escape pods then dangling from parachutes then bobbing in lifeboats
places no one wants to be before the catastrophe

IV.

resilience is an easy word for a hard work
teaching us nothing declutters our house
like having it burn and nothing sensitizes us
to the end of the world like having our
own world end and we can't really say
we've lost everything as long as
we can still *say* we've lost everything

V.

under a sky neither falling nor limitless
we have only one generation ship in us
and all of us in one generation ship
yet the sky keeps burning down
through all fault of our own

Harms of Aggregation

the poor of too many mouths
the rich of eating too much

if too many sunny beautiful days make drought
what do too many sunny beautiful people make

when having enough for everyone
is never enough for anyone

Copula for Mathematicians

(Twelve in Fives and Sevens)

Nought that stands for aught
    ought not to fall for
aught that stands for nought,
    yet because love—a number
that stands for nothing
    divided by a concept
that stands for everything
    —still counts for something,
the universe is barely
    chaperone distance enough
to keep space between
    zero and infinity.

Memory of Asteroids Near JPL

From shining mountains, Santa Ana winds
stampede down-canyon. Eucalyptus writhe,
Italian cypress bow, palm fronds rattle
and shake. Cars swerve as tumbleweeds
big as escape pods bound across freeways.

Dodging twig-bag asteroids, I am for a moment
a valiant starship captain, daring and escaping
collision and certain doom.

Again.

Insight Paradox

(To the memory of my brother, Jay)

self-healing bubble
to unpierceable forcefield—
response when asked "if
you're such a nobody why's
everyone out to get you?"

Context Dependent

internal workings
unknown, or post-crash witness—
which definition
of "black box" is best suited
to our AI conundrum?

When Encountering Somnambulism

don't wake us
don't shake us
don't take our screens away
don't offer us satire

confused
afraid we wake
to never sleep again
we might jump angry
we might lash out

from the loud brink
of the echoing abyss
call us back
by our own names

ease us round
walk us safe to bed
there to sleep and forget
this dream of waking
ever happened

How The Preterite Survives

Be small. Live underground. Eat anything.

If the history of mass extinctions teaches nothing else, it still teaches us
to survive by being omnivorous, subterraneous, inconspicuous.

And—if we choose to flee our burning spacecraft in a tin-can escape pod,
like rats of the Elect, unencumbered by that old collective, "man"?

Then beshrew our brains! Adaptability be damned.

Eden's Expressway

we're looking forward
to going back to
some place we've never been

back to the garden
counterclock wisdom
where only sundials toll

infinite looping
one-sided surface
nobody gets there from here

taking forever
to get to nowhere
Möbius highway again

Another Emergent Property

(after T.S. Eliot)

Epiphany coming, she thinks about the Magi. Were they watchers after heaven,
> like her? Did they recognize not only the lesser epiphany of the guiding star
> but also the greater epiphany of the star-child's appearance in flesh?

Knowing the water-sign constellations and the precession of the equinoxes,
> did they suspect that infant to be the Piscean avatar? Could they predict
> he would tell his fishermen disciples he would make them fishers of men?
> Or that he would work the miracle of loaves and fishes?

What might they make of Caesar's coin in the mouth of Jesus' fish, at Capernaum?
Or fish's mouth Fomalhaut and its planet Dagon, named for an
> ancient half-man, half-fish god, two millennia in their future?

The meteor astronomer sighs. Ideas, stars, comsats, all constellated by imagination.
> But which are legitimate, and which the easier phantasms called asterisms? Which the epiphanies, and which the delusions?
> Which the other way home, through this Babel of stars?

About the Author

Howard V. Hendrix is an award-winning writer of poetry, fiction, and nonfiction. Hendrix's first four published novels appeared from Ace Books: *Lightpaths*, *Standing Wave*, *Better Angels*, and *Empty Cities of the Full Moon*. His fifth novel, *The Labyrinth Key*, appeared from Ballantine Del Rey, as did his sixth novel, *Spears of God*. His most recent collection of shorter fiction is *The Girls With Kaleidoscope Eyes and Other Analog Stories for a Digital Age* (Fairwood Press 2019).

He is the author of several novelette chapbooks and over fifty short stories, the latter collected in six short story collections between 1990 and 2014. His numerous poems include many pieces in *Star*Line*, as well as the SFPA Dwarf Stars 2010 winner "Bumbershoot" and "Extravehicular Activity," which appeared in the April 2023 issue of *Scientific American*. He is also the author of many political essays, book reviews, and works of literary criticism.

His book-length nonfiction includes *The Ecstasy of Catastrophe*, *Reliable Rain* (with Stuart Straw), and several works on which he served as co-editor: *Visions of Mars* (with George Slusser and Eric Rabkin), *Bridges to Science Fiction* (with Gregory Benford, Gary Westfahl, and Joseph D. Miller), *Science Fiction and the*

Dismal Science (with Gary Westfahl, Gregory Benford, and Jonathan Alexander).

A past Western Regional Director and Vice President of the Science fiction and Fantasy Writers of America (SFWA), he is a recurring guest editorial writer for *Analog Science Fiction and Fact* and the *San Francisco Chronicle*. Hendrix also taught writing and literature for many years at California State University Fresno.

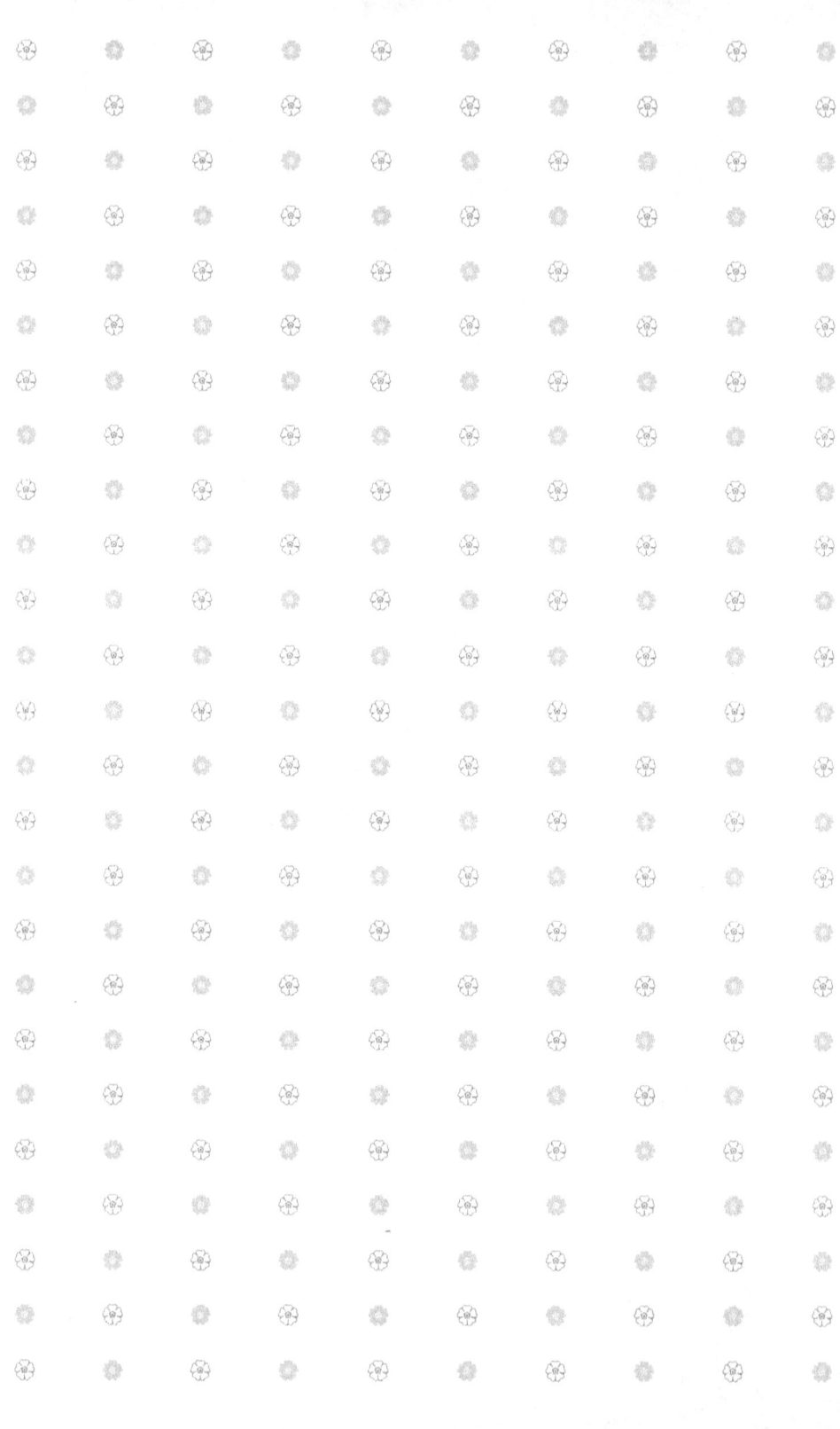

www.ingramcontent.com/pod-product-compliance
Lightning Source LLC
Chambersburg PA
CBHW020330010526
44107CB00054B/2055